DEPTH LEADS

WHY REAL LEADERSHIP STARTS ON THE INSIDE

Tanja Gruber

1st Edition, July 2025

www.tanjagruber.de
Publisher: ONDALY
ISBN Softcover: 978-3-903521-72-8
ISBN Hardcover: 978-3-903521-73-5
ISBN E-Book: 978-3-903521-74-2

Imprint:
ONDALY GmbH
Mariahilfpark 2
6020 Innsbruck
connect@ondaly.com
www.ondaly.com

Cover Design: Clélia Beck https://clesign.cc/

Disclaimer:
All information is provided without guarantee. The publisher and author accept no liability for any damage or disadvantage resulting from using the applications described in this book. You use everything at your own risk.

CONTENTS

Where do you stand?

I've often found myself right at the edge. And sometimes, life gave me that extra little push, and I ended up flat on the ground, deep down in the abyss. So what do you do when you've got no idea how to go on?

I probably wouldn't be alive today if I had stayed down.

Life kept throwing life-threatening challenges my way, and I had to look right at the stuff that hurt. No one goes to their limits voluntarily, you tend to turn back halfway, before things get tough, messy, or painful. But strength, healing, and power lie beyond the pain. It's only at the end of the slope that the wind shifts and lifts you up, and when you hit rock bottom, there's only one direction left: up.

Thanks to tons of trainings, books, and my own digging, I learned how to grow and stand up again and again, no matter what. That's how I found my own inner strength to lead and realized something important: real change always starts within. That's not something you learn in most leadership seminars, but you can learn it when you face your own shadows down in that inner abyss.

Being a strong leader and inspiring the people around you is something that matters, whether it's in your job or your personal life. It means being able to guide others and spark their inner drive to give their best.

Science shows that most of our perception and decision-making happens on a subconscious level. They say we only act consciously about five percent of the time, the rest happens on autopilot. Authors like Dr. Joe Dispenza, Dr. Ruediger Dahlke, Dr. John Bargh, and Dr. Bruce Lipton explain this really well in their work. And marketing's been taking advantage of it for ages: it knows the limbic system makes the decisions, while our rational side just comes up with excuses after the fact.

Because we run so much on unconscious patterns, every part of us we've pushed away, every shadow we've ignored, weakens our ability to lead effectively. People have a pretty good sense of whether you're at peace with yourself and being real. If you're not, communication gets tricky, especially since it's mostly nonverbal and unconscious, and working together ends up marked by mistrust. Nobody wants to follow someone who isn't clearly present.

So if you want to lead well, the first thing you've got to figure out is where you stand in life. Leadership starts with leading yourself. You make choices first and foremost for yourself. If you don't know where you are or where you're going, how can you make the right calls for anyone else?

It's like using a GPS: you need both your current location and your destination to find the best and fastest route. To build on what Lao Tzu once said: only when you know where you are **and** where you're headed can you find the path.

This book is here to help you become aware of your inner, unconscious burdens and tap into your own leadership power, so you can face tough situations in the outside world calmly and deal with them, the crises…

- …when your team, your employees, or the people by your side turn against you;
- …when you feel weighed down, even though everything looks like success on the outside;
- …when the pressure and expectations on your shoulders feel almost too much to bear;
- …when you're scared of what's ahead and ask yourself: Why?

In the first part of this book, I'm going to share my lowest points with you, honestly and openly. Then I'll show you some practical tools and ideas to help you turn your personal challenges, your headwinds, into strength and lift. Maybe you'll start seeing certain patterns, understand your own behavior better, or get a fresh perspective on yourself and your situation.

In the second part, I'll walk you through real-life examples from my coaching work, showing how facing your own shadows can bring light into dark times and seemingly hopeless situations. And in the third part, I'll give you tried-and-tested methods and exercises to help you figure out where you are right now and where you actually want to go.

Everything you'll read in this book is true, my truth. It's not based on scientific studies or research papers. It comes purely from my own experience and the knowledge I've gathered over many years.

All these little pieces, from what I've learned and lived, have come together to form a picture that's helped a lot of people in my coaching sessions build up their resilience and personal impact.

Part I

Experiencing darkness

—

Do I want to live or die?

In this part, you'll get a glimpse into my personal story as well as the stories of people I've worked with in my coaching sessions. Each of the six chapters will highlight certain patterns. Some of them might feel familiar to you, either from your own experience or from people around you. That's an important foundation for the second part of the book, where we'll dive into working with unconscious parts of your personality.

Heads-up, trigger warning: In this book, I speak openly about topics like violence, abuse, and sexuality. These are things many people are affected by, but they're still surrounded by a lot of societal taboos and hardly ever talked about.

That doesn't do anyone any favors. Because when these

things stay in the shadows, people end up pushing their fears deep into the unconscious. But just ignoring or denying them doesn't make them go away. On the contrary, they keep simmering in the background and slowly gain power, standing in the way of your personal growth. And often, you don't even realize what's holding you back.

That's exactly how it was for me…

Chapter 1
Birth trauma

My parents were young when they had me, probably too young, considering the tough childhoods they both went through. My mom was only 20 and didn't want a child yet. That might be why she spent a long time believing she just had issues with her appendix. It must have been a real shock when she finally realized she was pregnant. She was desperate and absolutely didn't want to have the baby. She wanted to get rid of me.

My parents never talked to me about any of this. It was only much later, during my desperate search for answers, trying to figure out why life kept throwing tougher and tougher challenges my way, that I started digging into all kinds of knowledge. One thing I came across was identity-oriented psychotrauma therapy (IoPT). This approach, developed by psychologist and psychotherapist Prof. Franz Ruppert, is based on the idea that trauma from early childhood, or even from before birth, can leave deep marks on a person.

Through lots of constellations, a method from systemic therapy, I was able to bring perceptions and memories from before, during, and after my birth out of my subconscious and into my awareness. That helped me make sense of things I hadn't been able to understand before.

Experiences before birth

My mom was carrying a child she absolutely didn't want. She did everything she could to get rid of me, even considered killing herself, just so she wouldn't have to become the mother of this "thing." But a fetus in the womb isn't a "thing." It already picks up on so much of what's going on around it. It feels what the mother does and senses what's going on inside her. Instinctively, it knows that its survival totally depends on the mother's well-being. And intuitively, it also knows it wants to live.

If the mother is close to ending the pregnancy or even her own life, the fetus feels pure terror, one of the most intense emotions there is. It becomes afraid of the mother, but also afraid for her. And these overwhelming feelings are just too much. The fetus can't handle them. The only way to survive is to split off from those feelings. In psychological terms, that's called dissociation.

That's exactly what I did. I stopped feeling my fear of dying. I made myself small in my mother's womb, pushed myself away, twisted myself around. For a long time, I wondered why I was born with a curved spine that still causes me health problems today. Now I think it goes back to that time in the womb, where I shaped myself into something just to stay alive. What I didn't ask myself for the longest time was why I didn't feel fear at all as a child.

Emotional dissociation

Where other kids were scared, I stayed calm. Even when I had serious accidents, I didn't feel any real fear. I didn't know what fear of dying felt like, I was completely cut off from it. But since I didn't realize that, I just assumed I wasn't scared because nothing ever really happened to me. Sounds crazy now, but even as the accidents kept piling up, I stuck to that belief. Not feeling fear was just normal for me, I hadn't recognized that I was dissociating.

By now, I've worked with many people in my coaching sessions who also couldn't feel their fear, instead, they felt emotionally numb. That lack of emotion shows up in all kinds of ways. Some people actively seek out dangerous situations just to feel something. A good example would be race car drivers or extreme athletes who constantly put themselves at risk.

Others push themselves past their limits by overworking, while many struggle because animals around them, maybe horses or pets, are tough to handle or often sick. Even children can mirror hidden inner conflicts, for example through frequent illness or difficult behavior. Health issues or accidents in general are signs that something inside us isn't in alignment with who we really are. The same goes for constant tension or problems with employees, colleagues, or customers, it's a clear signal to look inward and find the real cause behind the conflict.

When I work with people who were never meant to be born, who were supposed to be aborted, I often see the same thing: they can't seem to find their place in life. They don't really feel themselves and often struggle with low self-worth. In relationships, conflict is common, and they tend to take on the role of a passive observer, as if their own life doesn't really concern them. They often face setbacks, have trouble finishing projects, or they might be successful on the outside but don't actually feel happy about it.

This kind of dissociation or emotional numbness doesn't just affect fear, it blocks other strong feelings too. I never felt things like overwhelming joy, deep contentment, or intense anger, even though I saw others experience them. Those emotions were probably there in me too, but I just couldn't access them.

At the same time, I never learned how to feel safe in my own body. In the womb, a time when we're supposed to build a deep sense of physical safety, I experienced the opposite. I never knew what it felt like to be safe in my body.

But it took me decades to even realize that. That's one of the biggest problems with psychological trauma: most of it gets processed on a totally unconscious level, and the blocks it creates stay buried deep in the subconscious. They keep affecting us, and unless we actively work through them, they'll never come to light. And sometimes, those traumas don't even come from our own life…

Chapter 2
Family history

I never got to meet my maternal grandmother. And yet, or maybe because of that, I loved her deeply. Today, I think I understand why: a child who grows up without connection is desperately searching for love, even from someone they've never actually met.

The traumatic experiences that affected the women in my family line were never worked through or resolved, neither by my grandmother nor by my mother. So they were passed on to me.

My mother's early childhood was heavily burdened. My grandmother gave her away at a very young age. I was told that it was my grandmother's sister who brought her to her new foster parents by bicycle. The journey to their small village was over 50 kilometers long, and for a four- or five-year-old riding on the back of a bike, that must have been incredibly tough. And I'm sure my mother instinctively knew what was happening: that she would never see her birth mother again.

Her foster parents weren't able to have children of their own. They meant well and genuinely wanted to care for this traumatized little girl. But it quickly became clear they were in way over their heads. My birth grandmother had been a prostitute, and my mother had seen things as a child that no child, and really, no one, should ever have to witness.

For a long time, I had no idea what my grandmother had done for a living. Years later, I started looking into her life. What I found out was that her death had been just as troubled as her life. I was never able to figure out exactly how she died. There had been a police file on her, but the documents had been destroyed just six months earlier. It's very likely that my grandmother was murdered, though I also heard rumors she had starved to death.

During my research, I also discovered that my mother had a half-sister. Like my mom, her birth certificate listed the father as unknown. She wasn't placed with foster parents but ended up in an orphanage. Later in life, she worked in an institution herself and never really left that world of confinement. When I visited her a few years ago, she was in a wheelchair, severely overweight, and living in a care home. She, too, had never been able to free herself from the burden of the trauma that had been passed down. And sadly, my mother and aunt aren't isolated cases.

There's a lot of evidence showing that unresolved trauma and negative experiences can be passed down through as many as seven generations. Based on what I've seen in my own coaching work, I actually believe the chain can go back even further. After doing a family constellation session focused on my own lineage, I suspect that the trauma in the women of my family stretches way beyond seven generations.

These inherited emotions tend to hold on to their intensity and can affect later generations just as strongly as they did the original one. But the memory of the actual events fades more and more with each generation, which makes it harder for people down the line to trace the roots of their emotional struggles. These children end up living with the burdens of the past, and often they're emotionally just trying to survive, especially if there's no loving adult there to support and catch them. That, unfortunately, wasn't the case for me growing up.

Chapter 3
Childhood trauma

A baby's survival depends on being cared for, not just physically, but also emotionally and mentally. Deep down, the baby knows this. From the very beginning, a child relies on attention and care from an adult, and only that bond can give them the sense of safety they need to survive. If that care is missing, the child starts feeling fear of death, because it believes it will die without love.

When kids don't get love or are poorly cared for in those early years, they often spend their whole lives desperately searching for attention and affection. They also tend to be extremely sensitive to criticism or rejection. In my case, my mother left me alone very early on, and even hours of crying didn't change a thing.

After my parents got married and I was born, they first lived with my father's mother. But there were a lot of conflicts, so when I was two or three years old, they moved to a nearby village, where my sister was born.

When I was four, my father walked out, on the house and on his relationship with my mother. He emigrated to Saudi Arabia for work and only visited occasionally in the following years, although he did send money regularly. He probably sent enough, but my mother had never been good with money and couldn't manage with what she had. So she went back to work early on. She worked 30 hours a week as a saleswoman in a department store, plus weekends and sometimes evenings during the week.

The foster parents who had raised her often looked after me during that time. They basically became my foster-grandparents. I loved being with them, and it was always so much harder for me when they brought me back to my mother, where I'd be left alone again. Near their house, I also discovered a special place: the neighboring farm.

When I was five, I got to be around horses and cats for the first time. Finally, I met living beings I actually felt connected to, something I'd never experienced with people. The animals became a substitute for the love I didn't get from my mother, especially the horses. Even today, they still ground me and have saved my life more than once, although, to be fair, they've also put me in danger just as often. But more on that later.

Luckily, I had two good friends from neighboring villages who also lived on farms. I got to spend a lot of time with them, which helped me escape the loneliness at home and be around animals that I always felt truly loved by. Because I never really had emotional connection with people growing up, I still find it hard to form deep relationships today.

I know a lot of people who've gone through similar experiences and feel the same way I do. When you've grown up like that, it's often really hard to tell whether someone truly loves and accepts you. That's how constant conflicts can develop. Even if the partner is giving a lot of love, they can never fully make up for that emotional gap from childhood, so the person still feels unloved. On top of that, people like this often struggle with low self-esteem and constantly look to others for validation and proof of their worth.

The less love a child receives, the more desperately they seek ways to obtain it, both in childhood and later in life, and will do anything to achieve this. From early childhood, I was overwhelmed with duties and responsibilities by my mother, who was completely overwhelmed by her children and work. This is referred to as parentification in technical terms. As a result, I was never able to be a child, but I hoped that by fulfilling all my tasks I would receive love and affection from my mother, which unfortunately I never got from her.

Parentification and the associated childhood trauma and lack of self-esteem affect many people, some of whom I have met in my coaching sessions. It is often a great challenge to break out of the vicious circle of having to overburden oneself in order to prove one's worth, while already being under excessive pressure and stress.

To make matters worse, in addition to parentification, I also experienced abuse by my own father at an early age. In my youth, I was also the victim of sexual assault by a group of teenagers from the neighbouring village, who got me drunk, recorded the 'incident' and published the video. Worse than the act itself, however, was the reaction of my parents, who did not provide me with emotional support, but instead blamed me for the assault.

Because of these experiences, it was normal for me later on when my father returned to Germany and abused me emotionally. My mother had divorced him in the meantime and moved away with my sister. After I had already lived alone for two years as a sixteen-year-old because of this, my father returned from Saudi Arabia. We lived together in a small flat for about two years. During this time, he abused me as a substitute companion, substitute domestic help and substitute wife. We even slept in the same bed, although there were no further physical assaults. And I went along with it all because I had no awareness of what was actually going wrong.

These experiences in my childhood and youth have had a decisive impact on my relationships and my self-esteem: on the one hand, I love interpersonal contact with men because it gives me a feeling of connection and closeness. On the other hand, it is often difficult for me to recognise that men sometimes just want sex as a way of temporarily escaping from their relationships with their wives.

Chapter 4
Accidents

On April 19, 2015, a beautiful Sunday, perfect spring weather for a carriage ride, I had an accident that would change my life forever. Up until that moment, I was always able to perform, followed my career path, and earned a good living. But in one split second, everything changed for good.

The carriage driver had two calm horses hitched up and was sitting to my right. I had her six-year-old son on my lap. Her partner was supposed to sit in the back but was still standing next to the carriage. The moment she gave the horses the signal to go, things went terribly wrong.

One of the horses stepped out a bit faster than the other and hit the shaft with its leg. It got spooked and bolted, pulling the second horse with it. The carriage slammed into a telephone pole, which luckily just tilted to the side instead of falling over. The impact threw the carriage into a roadside ditch, crushing me and the panicked horse underneath. The child was thrown from the carriage but, miraculously, was mostly unharmed. The driver also got away with just minor injuries.

But I got the full impact: the entire weight of the carriage landed on me. When the driver's partner lifted it off, I somehow managed to crawl out myself. But then the horse, which he thought was dead, suddenly moved and freed itself. In the process, the carriage rolled over me a second time. When I was finally rescued, badly injured, the emergency doctor had me flown to a hospital by helicopter immediately.

The lead-up to the accident

You could call it a chain of unlucky coincidences: a normally calm horse spooked, I ended up under the carriage, and I was the only one seriously injured. But honestly, this accident fits perfectly into a long line of similar incidents, so I don't really believe it was just bad luck. The one good thing about that terrible accident was that it finally pushed me to start looking for the real cause behind all the accidents I'd had over the years.

The first one I remember was when I was a little kid playing up in the attic, and the closed trapdoor suddenly gave way under my feet. I fell down a whole floor, but my mother didn't think I needed to see a doctor. After that, there were countless accidents, especially with horses: one bit me on the butt, I tore my cruciate ligament in a fall, one horse reared up and injured my chin and tongue, another bolted, broke through a fence, and crushed me underneath. Horses gave me love and a sense of connection, but they also nearly cost me my life more than once.

That runaway horse incident really should have been a wake-up call, but I still wasn't ready. So life handed me a more serious warning on that fateful day in April. Interestingly, April 19th is the birthday of my horse Pascha, with whom I've always felt a deep connection. It's also the day I believe my mother tried to end her pregnancy with me.

In the accident, I broke several transverse processes in my lower spine, had fractures in my rib cage, a traumatic brain injury, and damage under one eye. The hospital recognized and treated those injuries properly. I was discharged pretty quickly and continued treatment as an outpatient. But three serious issues were missed: my hip had been knocked out of alignment from the carriage's weight, my right thumb was severely injured, with a crushed and dislocated joint and a torn ligament, and one of the carpal bones in my wrist had twisted and tilted.

That unstable hip still causes my knee to shift regularly, which is slowly threatening my ability to walk. The missed thumb injury and a botched follow-up treatment ended up costing me the base joint of my thumb. And the twisted bone in my wrist still gives me trouble, I'll be dealing with that for the rest of my life.

It took four weeks after the accident for doctors to even partially realize how bad the thumb injury was. After surgery to repair the torn ligament, the unbearable pain didn't go away. Eventually, they told me I'd need to fuse the joint using a metal plate. I tried everything to avoid that. I saw hand surgeons all over Germany, hoping to find another solution that didn't involve fusion.

But then the insurance company got involved. At first, they covered everything without issue. But later, they started putting pressure on me: either I had the joint fusion surgery right away, which is irreversible, or they'd stop all payments. Looking back, I wasn't in a state to make a clear decision. I was in constant pain and had no real options. So in September 2016, I went through with the operation.

Later, I found out that artificial thumb joints already existed at that time. But the implant would've been more expensive than the metal plate used for the fusion. If I had gotten the implant, the function of my thumb could've been preserved.

In 2018, the insurance company suddenly stopped making payments altogether. Before that, they had gradually begun denying smaller and smaller reimbursements. I had already hired a lawyer from the very beginning, but that didn't help. Eventually, I was given a choice: either accept a settlement or take them to court. My lawyer didn't offer much support, she clearly saw me as a case not worth her time, and the insurance company clearly wanted to get rid of me too.

So I was left to deal with the decision on my own. I was under constant pressure, in pain, and struggling with the lasting effects of my hand and hip injuries. Eventually, they raised the settlement amount a bit (without adjusting for inflation), but the final sum was nowhere near enough for someone who would never be able to work like before.

No one really cared what happened to me after that, not the caseworkers, not my lawyer, not the hand surgeon. I had to fight my way through it alone.

In 2019, I had the metal plate removed because I just couldn't stand the pain and the feeling that my thumb was being crushed by it. The severe misalignment of the thumb still causes extreme pain to this day. It feels like a foreign object, something broken I have to live with. It won't heal and will remain a constant trigger for the rest of my life.

But out of that dark and difficult place, I began focusing on finding the root causes, and on actively working through my trauma. I set out on an inner journey. That's how I learned to draw strength and resilience from trauma, and how to build real perseverance.

Chapter 5
Finding peace

Everywhere you look, people are getting into fights. Arguments often start over the smallest things. No one becomes happier by attacking someone else. And yet, people just can't seem to let each other be. Why is that?

In my own experience, it's because so many people are living in conflict with themselves. They reject parts of who they are, and that inner struggle keeps showing up in their lives until they finally become aware of it. If you're not at peace on the inside, it shows up on the outside. You push that awful feeling away to protect yourself, but the wound inside stays open.

It wasn't until after my serious accident that I really understood this. I had already been working on myself for years, trying to explore my own darkness. But it was that accident that forced me to go even deeper. I realized how much of myself I had been rejecting, especially my body, my injuries, and my weight. I hated not being able to do things the way I wanted.

I wanted nothing to do with those parts of myself. I was far from being at peace with who I was, in fact, I was at war with myself. And that inner rejection led to rejection from the outside, which hurt me deeply again and again. Eventually, I saw that the real conflict was inside me, and that change could only come from within. Just becoming aware of that shifted so much. The more I've been able to make peace with my own shadows, the more peace I've been able to bring into the world around me, that's what experience has taught me.

Before my accident, I faced a lot of rejection from men, mostly because of my weight. It always hit me hard and was something I really struggled with. But after the accident, once I started facing my fear of death and working through my trauma, something changed. I made peace with my body. And now, it's striking how often men tell me they love my curves during sex.

This brings us to the end of the first part of the book. So the question now is: how can we take the dark experiences in life and use them to grow, so we become stronger and more resilient on the inside?

Part II

Bringing things to light

–

Do I want to look or look away?

Every person carries both light and dark parts within them, and has responsibility for their own life. You can blame the outside world for the bad stuff that happens and wait until life forces you to take a closer look. Or you can make the choice to face your darker sides yourself and create real, lasting change from within.

Both the hard and the good experiences help you see yourself more clearly through what happens around you. And from there, you can grow, evolve, and get stronger. It's a chance to awaken and strengthen your inner leadership, so you can become a more authentic leader on the outside, both in your personal life and at work.

Chapter 6
The good in the bad

People are dual beings and carry all kinds of opposites within them: masculine and feminine traits, joy and pain, love and hate. These opposites can't really be separated, they belong together and blend into each other. There's a bit of light in every dark side, and a bit of darkness in every bright one.

The Taoist yin-yang symbol shows this in a powerful way: a circle made up of one black half and one white half. Right in the middle of the bright side is a black dot, and in the darkest black is a white dot.

Put simply, the white side stands for the good in life, and the black side for the bad, two forces that are deeply connected but still in total contrast. It mirrors life itself: nothing is ever just good or just bad. Every good thing comes with something difficult, and every hardship carries something good. They rely on each other, one can't exist without the other.

When we narrow our view to only the "positive" or only the "negative," it always leads to pain.

If everything around you feels dark and heavy, it becomes overwhelming, it can feel like there's no light left in the world at all. But only seeing the bright side isn't healthy either. It throws things off balance. You cling to the way things are and fear any kind of change. But as Albert Einstein famously said, life is all about change, it's like riding a bike: if you stop moving, you fall.

Pain always shows up when we cling too tightly to the good or try to suppress the uncomfortable. And that pain is what keeps us from finding inner peace. But when we have the courage to walk straight through that emptiness, we find something meaningful on the other side. We have to let go of all judgment and look at the bigger picture, the constant flow of change. That's how we reconnect with ourselves, with what's always been there, waiting to be seen.

In that state of inner peace, you realize that whatever situation you're in right now could already be different in the next moment. Everything is just an experience in the now, and then comes the next. In that presence, you feel your body more intensely than ever, while also noticing that your being goes beyond just the body.

Many cultures and religions call this sense of connection

spirituality or creative energy. You could also just see it as cosmic energy. Either way, inner peace is the place where you can create something new, be creative, come up with ideas, and inspire and uplift others.

Of course, it's not always easy to keep this mindset in everyday life. And that's okay, because life is what it is. And when we let life be just that, it brings peace. You start to notice the darkness within the light, and the light within the darkness, and accept both.

People are on different paths: some are fixated on their bright side and have cut themselves off from their darkness, while others are stuck in their dark side and can't see the light. Both kinds of separation cause pain. Both are missing a part of themselves, it's like standing on one leg. When too many experiences hit them, they topple over. Balance lies in the golden middle, in being aware of both the duality and the unity.

Chapter 7
The great wall

Over the past few years, I've had the chance to support many people as a coach. Some of the topics that came up again and again were conflicts with employees or clients, losing important contracts, constant stress, negative thought loops, overwhelm, or a lack of joy in what they were doing. A lot of the people I coached also felt stuck in life. Even though they seemed successful on the outside, they were unhappy with themselves, couldn't make decisions, or were struggling because their kids, or even the animals around them, were often sick, reflecting what was going on inside them.

Trauma walls

What all of them had in common: they didn't know why things were the way they were. And whenever they tried to figure it out, it felt like running into a wall inside themselves. These inner "trauma walls" are protective barriers and coping mechanisms that help a person survive emotionally, without them even realizing it. They usually form in response to painful or difficult experiences, what psychologists call trauma.

On my own journey inward, I learned a lot and went through many different trainings. That's how I eventually discovered identity-oriented psychotrauma therapy (IoPT). And honestly, I can say this method probably saved my life. IoPT gave me the tools to make peace with myself and grow as a person.

This method was developed by Prof. Franz Ruppert. He discovered that early childhood trauma has a huge impact on people. These traumas split the psyche, and the split remains until a person is willing to confront and integrate those disconnected parts of themselves. The triggering experiences are buried so deep in the unconscious that people don't remember them at all. They're just left wondering why they can't seem to get along with themselves or the world the way others do.

According to Prof. Ruppert, there are different kinds of trauma. People, especially children, often react to them with dissociation, as we've already talked about. Two key types he identifies are developmental trauma and attachment trauma.

Developmental trauma happens when a child can't go through their natural developmental steps. This might be because the parents are dealing with unresolved trauma of their own and can't really take care of themselves, let alone their child. Instead of healing their fears, they pass them on.

Attachment trauma, on the other hand, happens when a child is rejected or turned away by their main caregiver.

Since a baby is completely dependent on the care of an adult, any kind of emotional rejection feels life-threatening.

According to Prof. Ruppert, there's not just the traumatized part of the psyche and the protective mechanisms, what he calls the "survival part", but also a healthy part that always remains. That healthy part helps build a stable identity and supports your inner drive and strength.

When someone experiences several types of trauma at once, Prof. Ruppert calls it **complex trauma**. With complex trauma, it becomes even harder to figure out where your feelings actually come from. It's like a ball of yarn made up of different threads, you have to slowly and patiently untangle it to see which emotion belongs where.

Physical trauma can also lead to psychological trauma, and the other way around. That's because the body and the mind aren't separate, they constantly affect each other. Maybe one day I'll write a book about my own experiences and thoughts on the connection between body, mind, and soul.

A strong sense of identity, your own will, and a willingness to take responsibility for your life are key to unraveling that emotional ball of yarn. That's how you can make better decisions and learn to accept and integrate every part of yourself, including the wounded shadow parts.

Over the course of my coaching work, I've seen some real breakthroughs, moments where people truly transformed at a deep level.

Chapter 8
The reclamation

Why is it so important to reconnect with yourself and your emotions, and figure out where they actually come from? Because only when you truly know yourself can you make the right decisions for yourself and others. Pure logic can't do that. Decision-making is actually an emotional process that usually happens unconsciously and isn't just based on facts and logical arguments. There's a reason people say, "Go with your gut."

But what if you don't have access to your emotions, or you don't trust what you feel, because it doesn't seem to make sense logically?

Think back to the image of the ball of yarn made of emotions: at first glance, you can't really tell where all the threads come from, whether they're yours, tied to your own past trauma, or inherited from earlier generations. It's only when you start untangling the yarn, bit by bit, that you can unravel those knots and reclaim your emotional world.

To do that, you first need to connect with what you're currently feeling and figure out where it comes from and what's behind it. In a way, it's like you need to look over your own shoulder and observe yourself from a distance. Since that's not physically possible, we use a tool instead: a mirror. IoPT has developed a method that works just like a mirror, it's called **intention work**.

Intention work

Intention work can be done either one-on-one with a therapist or in a group, and it works like this: you come up with a sentence, a question, or an image that reflects whatever is currently weighing on you, that's your intention.

Ideally, the intention should include an "I" or something close to it, like "me" or "my." You're totally free to choose your own wording. Some examples might be:

- Who am I as a leader?
- What's really behind the conflict with my employee?
- What can I do to help the company reach this goal?
- Why do I keep losing client contracts?
- What's draining my motivation?
- How am I perceived as a leader?
- How can I lead my team efficiently?
- How can I find clarity within myself about what the next good step for the company is?
- How can I motivate and support the team in the best possible way?

- How can I find clarity within myself about what long-term goals should be set?
- What decisions can I make to improve customer satisfaction?
- How do I recognize unhealthy structures in the company?
- How do my decisions impact the company?
- How can I communicate upcoming changes to my team in a way that leads to high acceptance?

You're allowed to bring up anything, and honestly, the exact wording of the intention doesn't matter all that much during the actual process. What's really fascinating about IoPT is what's behind the stated intention: What experiences led to it? What emotions are buried deep in the subconscious and start rising to the surface through the intention?

Once you've come up with or drawn your intention, people from the group are chosen to act as "representatives" or "resonance givers." These people tune in to each word or image in your intention, emotionally stepping into those roles and expressing what they feel or sense.

Everyone then decides for themselves what parts of that resonate with their own life and what fits their personal story. The goal is to understand what inner forces are at work and why you've become the person you are today. This has a big impact on your ability to lead, both as a leader and as an entrepreneur, and it strongly shapes the kinds of business decisions you make.

Through your representatives, who tune in to you and your intention, a completely new perspective opens up, like being able to look over your own shoulder, which isn't something you can do on your own. That mirror gives you access to feelings you might still be cut off from, even if at first, you're not yet able to fully feel them.

How long it takes for those feelings to come back varies from person to person. For some, it happens quickly. For me, it took a while before I could not only recognize my buried fear of dying but also really connect with it emotionally. Feeling it is the first step toward understanding and accepting it.

Using this and other ways of working through trauma and finding yourself, you can reclaim your inner experience and begin to understand and integrate the parts of your personality you've pushed away. Fully accepting all of those hidden parts is a key theme, and often the biggest challenge, in healing trauma. It's a lifelong journey. Each insight opens the door to new experiences and lessons that weren't possible before. And with every step, you get closer to the healthy, empowering part of your true self.

Conscious conflict resolution in companies

After diving deep into trauma and its many effects in this chapter, I now want to show you how all of this relates to you and your role as a leader.

As mentioned earlier, we always lead "human to human." That means every decision a leader makes impacts other people, and the whole company. The more aware a leader is of the conscious and unconscious forces at play within themselves, the better they can make decisions and set a clear course.

We live in a society that focuses heavily on performance and outward results. There's little talk about inner awareness or what's really going on inside, and psychological issues often go completely unaddressed. Because of this, it's pretty safe to say that trauma, in some form, affects all of us, especially since unresolved trauma tends to be passed down through generations.

A company itself never makes decisions, it's always the people behind it. And those people come with their own forces, needs, wishes, and values. Employees, business partners, customers, they all bring their own layers into the mix. This kind of unconscious interaction isn't something we can fully grasp with our rational minds, it mostly plays out beneath the surface. Still, there are ways to make at least parts of it more visible. And the more we can feel what's going on beneath the surface, the more options we open up that we didn't even know were there.

Here's an example: A business owner gets into a conflict with his secretary. He makes a careless comment, which she takes personally. But she doesn't feel comfortable bringing it up. So the unprocessed emotion lingers in her. She starts to lose her openness and neutrality toward her boss, and their working relationship suffers. If this conflict isn't addressed, and depending on what's happened before, it could eventually lead to her quitting, either emotionally or officially.

Ideally, it's up to each person to work through their own emotions and communicate openly. But a lot of people don't realize they have that responsibility. Instead, they project their inner emotional world onto others, in this case, the secretary onto her boss. If the business owner lacks the sensitivity to notice that something's off, the tension just sits there, unspoken, and slowly harms the company.

But if the boss starts becoming aware that something in the relationship with his secretary doesn't feel right, he can take the initiative to talk about it. That kind of conscious approach can resolve the conflict, and save him a lot of time, money, and stress by not having to hire and train someone new.

Another example from intention work clearly shows the benefits of conscious conflict resolution in a business setting: A customer is unhappy with a decision the business owner made. But that dissatisfaction isn't openly communicated, and the owner has no idea the customer is upset. If the conflict goes unnoticed and unresolved, the company will very likely lose a good client.

But if the business owner develops a better sense for the relationship, they can respond differently, and probably keep the client instead of losing them. This kind of increased awareness of interpersonal dynamics can save a lot of time, money, and energy. It helps the business keep a valuable customer, instead of having to go out and find a new one.

Delegating on the inner path to success

At the top of a company, the focus is usually on looking ahead, direction, future, growth. But inner perfectionism and the mindset of needing or wanting to do everything yourself can often trip you up. If you want people to be genuinely drawn to what your company offers, you first need to feel good about yourself, because trusting relationships with customers only happen when you're at peace with yourself.

The kind of self-reflection needed here can start with questions like: Are there parts of me that believe I have to do everything on my own, because I think I can do it better than others, or because I'm afraid too many mistakes will happen if I delegate?

This inner mindset creates constant internal pressure and the feeling of never being enough. The result: you end up working in your business instead of on it. At the same time, you're sending your team the message that you don't really trust them. In my experience, that often leads to employees just going through the motions instead of taking initiative or thinking strategically. But motivation and performance can only grow when employees are trusted and given space to be creative.

Mistakes are part of being human, if you don't accept that, you just create more pressure and more mistakes.

These fears, not trusting others and needing to do it all yourself, are often rooted in early attachment patterns. The following intention statements can help leaders learn to accept mistakes, in themselves and others, and develop a greater willingness to delegate tasks:

- How can I learn to trust my team more?
- How can I get better at delegating tasks?
- What fears are at play in me when I feel like I have to do everything myself?

In my work with leaders, one thing keeps coming up: teamwork and making decisions together are among the biggest challenges in companies. In many teams, there are hidden, unspoken conflicts bubbling beneath the surface, and instead of working together toward a goal, people are unconsciously working against each other. These tensions usually go unnoticed and unaddressed. As a result, a company's success can be blocked from the inside, without any obvious reason on the outside.

The causes for this can vary: personal goals of individual team members that unconsciously take priority over the company's goals, unresolved relationship issues within the team, and so on. Here are some examples of intention statements that can help explore this:

- How can I recognize the hidden conflicts within the team?
- How does the team relate to the company's goal, and what about each individual member?
- Who am I within the team?

Inner and outer values

Especially in the service industry, it's often not just the actual offer that makes the sale, but also which personalities come together, and what kind of feeling that creates for the potential or existing customer. Emotional resonance plays a key role here. Still, in many businesses, the reason behind a buying decision is often searched for in surface-level factors. The emotional side is ignored, which, in my experience, is a big mistake. People make buying decisions unconsciously within the first few seconds. As the saying goes:

You never get a second chance to make a first impression.

Marketing research confirms this: all the product explanations that come after that first impression are just there to satisfy our rational mind. Some useful intention statements for exploring this area might be:

- How can I figure out what emotions our product or service triggers in our customers?
- How do I personally feel about this product or service?
- What emotions do I want to spark in my ideal customer with this product or service?

What all of this makes clear is this: clear thinking isn't enough, we also need to create clear emotions and connect with people on a feeling level. That requires inner clarity and coherence. In this sense, each of us is called to grow personally and keep working on ourselves. That's what I see as true self-development, a lifelong process that comes from within.

Chapter 9
Everything wants to be loved

Most people naturally prefer the path of least resistance. We want the good stuff in life, the things that feel nice and comfortable. The unpleasant, painful, or unfamiliar stuff? We'd rather ignore it. And that applies not just to our own lives, but also to how we relate to others. But what effect does that have on us?

Because our society is so focused on the external, it's pretty safe to assume that almost everyone today carries around unresolved or inherited trauma to some degree. Trauma, in this context, simply means injury, both physical and emotional. Even purely physical injuries always affect our mind and psyche too.

Some people carry more trauma, some less. But very few are willing to admit it. Trauma is often only associated with major events, like abuse, accidents, or violence. But trauma can start small. Even just experiencing strong rejection or disapproval can have a deep psychological impact, especially when you consider that, from an evolutionary standpoint, our survival as social beings has always depended on being accepted by the group. Emotions triggered by rejection often operate under the surface but still strongly influence how we behave around others.

Think about how often rejection happens at work. Depending on how well we know ourselves and how much we've explored our inner world, that rejection can act as a powerful unconscious trigger, and shape our reactions and decisions without us even realizing it.

As feeling, dual human beings, we all carry both healthy and wounded (or traumatized) parts of ourselves. The more aware we are of which part is steering our thoughts, emotions, and actions in any given moment, the more clarity and freedom we gain when making decisions. That doesn't just help us feel better personally, it also supports the greater good, like the well-being of a company. Because let's be real: only when the decision-maker is in a good place can they make good decisions for their business.

This is something I see over and over again in my work as a coach: How can someone who's (unconsciously) acting from their wounded inner child make decisions that are truly forward-thinking, for the company and everyone involved? If we want to grow in a meaningful and sustainable way, as a company or as a society, I believe there's no way around it: we have to face the trauma that still lives inside us and learn to lovingly accept even the unconscious or unwanted parts of who we are.

Exploring the Facets

I believe that every person has a kind of life mission to explore in all its facets. Life sends each person exactly the right situation or challenge for the "research task" that needs to be solved right now. But it's up to each individual whether they want to accept this learning task or not.

Sometimes, one doesn't recognize the task as such. As long as a person is disconnected from their own inner emotional world, this is quite likely. Intuitively, challenging situations are rejected and external reasons for problems are sought, and usually found, in their place. Conflicts are sometimes avoided unconsciously, sometimes consciously, and overall, the person is unhappy with life. But this only harms themselves.

Dissatisfaction and resistance to change cost a lot of energy, the constant attempt to fight these things externally. People try with all their might to put a lid on the dark parts of their personality and experiences to escape them. But the pressure in this boiling pot of experience keeps rising until, inevitably, one will be overwhelmed by it.

This energy is much better spent by at least making an attempt to accept difficult situations as challenges and to get to know oneself better in the process, even if it is sometimes painful.

Moreover, there is a saying: "What you shout into the forest echoes back." Whenever you judge others, you're really judging yourself, you reject externally what you reject internally in yourself. Since our brain and subconscious cannot distinguish between what we actually perceive and what we merely believe we perceive, it takes all judgments and evaluations personally. Thus, with every negative judgment of others, you reinforce inside yourself the feeling that you yourself are not right or good enough.

Everything about oneself, everything in this world, wants and deserves to be accepted and loved. Everything that is excluded makes life poorer: If you don't allow hate, you also can't allow love, and vice versa. Only when you learn to accept situations without judgment do you gain control over your decisions. Do you go into the anger or do you just notice it, without suppressing it, and then let it go?

Indecisive

People often struggle to make decisions because they fear making mistakes. Since mistakes are generally not accepted by society, this fear paralyzes them until others or circumstances make the decision for them. Then people often feel controlled by others and unhappy with the decision, but in many cases, they are actually responsible themselves.

A person's ability and joy in making decisions change dramatically once they let go of judgments and evaluations. "Regardless of how I decide, the outcome will be an experience for me. And every experience is valuable because I can learn from it. Everything that comes is lovable." With this mindset, making any decision suddenly becomes much easier.

Chapter 10
All the Misunderstood Returns

Life constantly sends messages, it wants to support our growth. What happens when we ignore these messages?

Messages of Life

Quite simply: Life sends you messages again, just a little clearer this time. It's not meant to annoy or torment you, rather, it's an opportunity for you to work on and resolve the issues that are currently important for you.

That's why it doesn't give up. But as long as you ignore these messages, you'll receive them in increasingly clearer forms, in the hope that you can no longer ignore them. The way these messages are delivered can vary widely. Illnesses often serve as messengers.

Physical complaints, on the one hand, become impossible to overlook after a certain point, but on the other hand, in Western society, they are often easily, or seemingly easily, treated. Responsibility for the suffering is passed to the doctor, who is expected, usually with a symptom-focused system of medication and operations, to make it disappear.

A typical example is heart problems that become increasingly severe. Medication or surgery to temporarily relieve symptoms is a personal decision, but it should always be accompanied by psychological analysis and exploration of the complaints to identify and address the actual cause, which may be psychosomatic.

Body and mind are closely linked. Especially the heart, one of the most important organs responsible for all life within us, is often affected. When a person has experienced emotional wounds, the heart can become a messenger that this person should take care of the consequences of these wounds to heal on a holistic level.

Illnesses as messages can appear both in people or in animals close to them. For some diseases, like laminitis in horses, it's often difficult to determine the cause from a conventional medical perspective. From another perspective, there may be a good explanation: Horses and animals in general very often take on the emotional burden their humans carry. Animals are very sensitive and perceptive, so the suffering of their human caregivers often expresses itself in them. In this way, they become carriers of the message for that person.

In my coaching practice, I've experienced multiple times how the moment the owner of a horse opened up to their own fears, the laminitis suddenly improved. I also witnessed this with my own horse Pascha, who one day happily came to me in the stable after months of being unable to walk due to laminitis and when I was close to ending his suffering. This happened the day after a session in which I reconnected with my fear of death, this time on a very deep level.

Messages from life are not limited to the physical level. Accidents are also an expression of the inner world showing up outside. My many accidents are an example: because I stubbornly refused to acknowledge my dark sides, my accidents kept getting worse. Today I wonder how it was possible that I simply repressed the clearest warning signs. Shortly before the carriage accident, I narrowly escaped a dangerous collision with a car while riding out with Pascha. I had received the call to change something in my life but apparently hadn't understood it yet.

Perhaps my story can serve as guidance to recognize and consciously explore the more subtle messages life sends. A married entrepreneur couple who came to my horse-assisted coaching was able to avert an impending crisis in their business this way.

They ran a manufacturing business together and constantly fought at work. The situation worsened steadily, but they suspected that an important message was underlying this ongoing conflict, and they were willing to look at it.

The friction point in their arguments was always the same: He was a man of quick decisions and preferred to accept a wrong decision rather than think things through calmly. She was the complete opposite: She thought ten times before feeling really sure about a decision.

In my coaching, I had them lead a horse without a halter in the round pen. A round pen is a large fenced circle where a horse can move freely but cannot run away. My horse Pascha is used to this “work circle” and generally feels comfortable there.

At first, leading the horse didn’t work at all: The horse either stopped or moved in a different direction than the couple. The animal could sense that each wanted to lead it in a different way. Accordingly, it was confused, didn’t know whom to follow, or refused.

Then I asked both to consciously realize that they obviously didn’t trust each other to be able to lead successfully in their own way. For the second attempt, they were to focus on internally accepting and appreciating the other’s leadership style.

The result of this internal perspective shift was immediately visible: Suddenly the horse walked peacefully between the two, they managed to lead the animal together. A few months later, the couple confirmed that since this experience, many things in their professional and private relationship had sustainably improved.

Chapter 11
Inner stress

How many people never suffer from stress? Most people today feel stressed and perceive the world as hectic and sometimes overwhelming. This stress can become a chronic condition. Chronic stress leads to exhaustion and fatigue and can also have physical consequences for health.

Constant tension

The reason lies in the fact that stress signals the nervous system with the highest tension, life danger. Chronic stress constantly drains the body's resources as it tries to cope with what it perceives as a life-threatening situation. Unlike traditional fight-or-flight reactions, like when a tiger appears, you often cannot fight or flee from the modern "tiger." These are often ongoing stresses, a constant tension that the body cannot process or resolve with its tiger-based stress response. The energy tied up in this way is then missing in other areas of life, creating a vicious cycle.

I once had a young entrepreneur in my horse-assisted coaching. He was visibly under pressure but hadn't come to me primarily because of that. He complained that although he could win many customer contracts, they often fell through again. He wanted to understand why.

I brought him together with my horse in the round pen. In this calm, protected environment, I let them connect. I stood at the edge, attentively observing.

The young man clearly couldn't build a connection with the horse: the animal repeatedly invited him to play, but he, in his intense tension, didn't notice these invitations. Chronic stress had caused the man to dissociate from his feelings and he couldn't perceive either his own or the horse's emotions.

How does chronic inner stress develop? In such cases, stress doesn't arise as a response to an external event, like a tiger appearing. Instead, the reaction is triggered by individually different stressors: something seemingly harmless outside awakens memories of a past injury, financial strain, a suppressed personality aspect, or a long-disconnected feeling. The body then triggers a normal physical stress response, but the adrenaline released isn't used up to solve the situation, through fight or flight, and thus remains. This puts strain on the physiological system and can lead to numerous direct and indirect health consequences.

Because the reaction happens unconsciously, those affected mistake the harmless trigger for the actual cause of the problem and complain about unfair circumstances, unwilling customers, and stubborn partners. But blaming others only increases the stress, making the person feel even more powerless because they give up responsibility for their emotional state and look for answers outside themselves. They take everything happening around them personally and believe the whole world is against them. They see themselves as victims, and a victim can only react, not act. This keeps them trapped in a stress loop.

Often, the other person's behavior has completely different (underlying) reasons that actually have nothing to do with the individual, and it just happens to hit their stressors or trigger points by chance. Only the individual themselves can work on these trigger points; no one else can change them. Lasting change and relaxation must begin within you.

After the first session with the entrepreneur and the horse in the round pen, I learned in conversation that he had been abused as a child. He had never processed this traumatic experience and was therefore disconnected from his feelings and fears. Once he recognized and felt this, I brought him back to the horse in the round pen. Now they walked side by side peacefully and moved in circles together.

The head of a naturopath school also asked me for help: He felt that nothing was moving in his relationship, which he didn't understand and which caused him great tension because he loved his wife.

I also brought him into the round pen with my horse. I asked him to open up to his feelings and then lead the horse in a circle without a halter. He tried hard, but the animal stood still. He tried coaxing and pleading, nothing helped: For a full hour, the horse didn't move. I had never seen Pascha like that before.

Finally, I suggested the man consciously feel what the paralysis inside him felt like, how it felt that nothing was moving in his relationship. When he truly connected with this feeling, and didn't just think about it, the paralysis inside him dissolved. Immediately, the horse also broke free from its freeze and willingly followed him. The inner stress about his partnership had blocked both him and the horse as a mirror on the outside. He had to recognize and loosen the tension inside himself to get things flowing again.

Chapter 12
Unpeace and War

Inner tensions, rejection, dissatisfaction, and anger show up on the outside. People project their own suppressed parts of their personality outward, where they try to fight against them with all their might, unsuccessfully, because they're looking for a solution in the wrong place.

Just like in small things, the big conflicts in this world are a reflection of the inner unrest people carry inside. This shows up as anger and aggression, but also as a hunger for power. Since many people have given up control over their own emotions and refuse to take responsibility for their lives, they try to gain power over others to keep them small as stand-ins for their own fears. This illusion of control serves to avoid feeling their own inner helplessness.

Misguided anger and hunger for power are the breeding ground where conflict, fights, and wars arise. Acting out anger outwardly can never soothe the anger within. From my perspective, there is only one path to more peace in the world: more and more people learning to work on their inner peace. The more people find peace within themselves, the less they need to carry their unrest outward. They resolve conflicts within themselves instead of projecting them onto others, and they learn empathy. Peace inside leads to peace outside. This is also clearly reflected in companies.

Even when one individual works on their inner peace, it immediately affects their environment. The more peace there is among employees and the workplace atmosphere is shaped by appreciation, respect, and goodwill, the more productive and valuable the company functions naturally. I see this again and again in my work as a coach: employees feel more connected to the company and willingly contribute their work. Inner resignations happen much less often, too.

This is the end of the second part. In the next part, I want to introduce practical exercises that can support anyone in courageously mastering challenges and hurdles, and on the other side of pain, finding themselves. Because through active engagement with one's own inner emotional world and the realization that true change and power lie within, anyone can develop inner strength and become an authentic leader.

Part III

Soaring After the Fall – Crises as opportunities for Growth

The third part of this book introduces 21 exercises across 7 different topics. These exercises help you gain more clarity about your own emotional world and lead yourself more consciously, so you can then show true leadership on the outside. Because we always radiate what's inside us, even especially the things we aren't aware of ourselves.

The following exercises support you not only in helping yourself but also the people in your professional or private environment:

- Employees will trust you more as an entrepreneur or

leader and follow you more willingly;

- You'll get along better with your colleagues and business partners;
- You'll inspire potential customers more and keep your existing ones;
- You'll build private relationships more calmly and maintain them over time.

In fact, life outside becomes easier when you come to terms with yourself, and these exercises help you get there.

A guide

It's important to do these exercises in a quiet place where you won't be disturbed and won't feel rushed. There's no need to hurry, in fact, quite the opposite: Working through questions that lead you to yourself, sometimes through painful experiences, is a challenge for both body and mind. Take your time and work at your own pace, regular, repeated practice is far more important than quick, short-lived results. Every step forward in this work expands your perspective and opens up new insights.

All your answers should be written down, because it makes a big difference to the brain whether we just think words or actually write them out. Putting things into written form lightens the mind, especially when you write by hand.

You can copy and fill out the exercises as templates from this book, but it's even more effective if you write the questions by hand on a blank sheet. This way, the questions affect both your body and mind at the same time.

I really want to encourage you to do these exercises again and again. Maybe you want to get a nice notebook to collect your answers or work with loose sheets that you bind together later. What's important is to get moving and let the energy flow so that change can happen.

Chapter 13
Life experiences

Some experiences in life can be a big challenge. But once you manage to change your perspective and see the situation as a learning opportunity, you lay the foundation to take responsibility for your inner emotional world and make lasting change possible.

Then you can analyze the stress, tension, fear, or anger, and figure out what you need to react differently and make different decisions the next time life tests you.

Exercise 1

Seeing what is and what can be

Recall a situation that was difficult for you. Write down the following points one after another:

1. What felt off or didn't sit right with me in this situation?

2. What emotions did I notice inside myself?

3. Where else do I know these emotions from?

4. What would have helped me stay grounded in myself during this situation?

Exercise 2

Cleanse your soul once a day

Just like brushing your teeth every day, it's helpful to do something good for your soul at least once a day. These can be small things that don't take much time, so they can really fit into your daily routine.

The important thing is to consciously take a moment to, for example, feel the spring sun on your skin, do nothing for five minutes, or let your thoughts drift away like clouds in the sky.

Write down here what nourishes your soul:

Exercise 3

I know you: you're my stress!

Recall a situation when you were stressed. Give this feeling of stress space and time. Then answer the following questions:

1. When I listen to myself: What might be behind this stress?

____ 1

____ 2

____ 3

2. Is there an experience this situation reminds me of?

____ 1

____ 2

____ 3

3. What would have helped me recognize, even in the original situation, that I was stressed, even though there was no objective reason outside?

____ 1

____ 2

____ 3

You should repeat this exercise often: It will sharpen your conscious awareness. Over time, you'll soon be able to recognize what triggers your tension in new stressful situations. This way, you'll be more and more able to consciously choose to resist stress.

Chapter 14
Waste of energy

When you complain about someone or something, you give the stressor your life energy. This turns it into a real problem, without actually getting any closer to a solution. The situation itself isn't the problem, it's more a reflection of a suppressed part of your own personality that you reject inside. So a problem-focused mindset drains an incredible amount of energy that then goes missing elsewhere.

The exercises in this chapter are meant to help you look at life from a solution-focused perspective, so that over time, when emotions run high, you can make different choices: Do you want to make the problem bigger or find a solution?

Exercise 4

Do I choose a problem or a solution?

Recall as many challenging situations in your life as possible. Note in which situations you thought problem-focused and in which you thought solution-focused.

1. Here I thought problem-focused:

______________________________ 1

______________________________ 2

______________________________ 3

2. Here I thought solution-focused:

______________________________ 1

______________________________ 2

______________________________ 3

3. What characterized the situations where I thought solution-focused?

______________________________ 1

______________________________ 2

______________________________ 3

4. What would I have needed to think solution-focused in the other situations?

______________________________ 1

______________________________ 2

______________________________ 3

This exercise also works well as a journal practice, where you record the day's events every evening and reflect on them.

Exercise 5

Finding peace

This exercise comes from dance therapy: Imagine you're sitting in a room full of people. Some of them are making noise while you're trying to find calm. Write down your ideas on how you could still manage to find peace.

Find at least 20 ways:

1

2

3

4

5

6

7

8

9

10

11

12

13

14

15

PS: Try out these ideas in your everyday life as well.

Exercise 6

Image check

Let any situation come to mind where you felt annoyed. Look closely, feel into it, and put yourself in that moment.

1. Describe the situation as precisely as possible. What happened?

2. Describe the thoughts that went through your mind:

3. Describe the images that came up inside you:

4. Describe exactly what annoyed you about it:

____________________ 1

____________________ 2

____________________ 3

____________________ 4

____________________ 5

Also observe yourself as you write your answers: What changes or shifts do you notice in yourself?

Chapter 15
Your loving self

Everyone gets tasks in life that lead to personal growth and development. Our wishes and dreams are the best guides to help us navigate the often challenging situations we face. These can be big wishes, like a big trip, success in business, more time with family, or small wishes, like a nice evening with your partner, a trip to nature, or a relaxed Sunday morning.

But in everyday life, we often overlook our wishes, there's always something else to do that seems "more important." We get used to putting our needs aside, which lowers our healthy self-worth. In this chapter, I'll introduce exercises to help you put yourself back, or for the first time, at the center of your life.

Exercise 7

Wish Concert

Write down all your wishes and dreams that you haven't (yet) been able to experience, maybe because it wasn't financially possible, or because you gave priority to other things. Give all your dreams space without holding back: the small ones, the big ones, and everything in between!

Exercise 8

No-Consequences

Write down the consequences of continuing to put your wishes and needs behind those of others.

1. What effects does this have on you?

2. What effects does this have on others?

Exercise 9

Yes-Consequences

Write down the consequences of giving your wishes and needs more importance than before.

1. How does that affect you?

2. How does that affect others?

Chapter 16
Goal setting

What kind of life do I want to live? Where am I now, and where do I want to go? How can I get there? What meaning do I find in life? These are important questions to help you make decisions that truly fit you and to develop inner leadership strength.

In my opinion, it helps to ask yourself from time to time: "Why am I here in this world?" The following exercises are designed to help you uncover what really matters to you in life, and to discover what kind of legacy you want to leave behind.

Exercise 10

Meaningful time

For an entire month, gather your thoughts about what the meaning of your life might be. Whenever something comes to mind, write it down right away. You could carry a notebook with you, email yourself from wherever you are, or jot down your ideas on your phone to write them here later.

Exercise 11

The eulogy

Imagine you are a silent guest at your own funeral. You listen to five people who come to your grave and say a few words about you and your life. Who steps forward? What does each person say?

Person 1: ____________________

Person 2: ____________________

Person 3: ____________________

Person 4: ____________________

Person 5: ____________________

Exercise 12

Reality check

How do you want the people around you to perceive you here and now? What do you wish for? Write down your answers for the important people in your life: your partner, family, employees, colleagues, etc.

Person 1: ____________________

____ 1

____ 2

Person 2: ____________________

____ 1

____ 2

Person 3: ____________________

____ 1

____ 2

Person 4: ____________________

____ 1

____ 2

Person 5: ____________________

____ 1

____ 2

If you're brave, let these people check how well your wishes match their perceptions.

Chapter 17
Good leadership inspires action

Being able to lead others in a way that they willingly move with you and follow you is a big part of success in life, both professionally and personally. Entrepreneurs and leaders, but also anyone who wants to inspire people for themselves or a cause, know this.

The most important prerequisite for good leadership is knowing and leading yourself well. Every split-off, every suppressed dark part of your own personality affects the effectiveness of your leadership. People can sense whether someone is authentic or not.

In my view, horses are the best mirror for your personal "leadership state." As herd animals, they're especially sensitive to whether the person trying to lead them radiates clarity, or is just pretending and sending mixed signals unconsciously. If a horse senses this inner conflict, it will resist, just like employees, customers, or partners resist when they get a bad feeling.

If you don't have a horse to help with the following exercises, you can alternatively work with a dog or a trustworthy, sensitive person who's independent from you. Your counterpart will immediately reflect back what's going on inside you and show how things change when you shift your inner attitude.

But in my experience, working with a horse is the most intense experience, so I describe the next three exercises in a setting supported by horses.

Exercise 13

Understanding your own leadership behaviour

This exercise helps you better understand your own body language and leadership skills. Do it with a horse in a safe space, like a round pen or indoor arena. Ideally, do this under the guidance of an experienced horse coach or therapist who can professionally support you. Feel free to have someone film you so you can observe yourself from the outside as well. Follow these steps and later write down your impressions:

1. Observe and Understand: Watch the horse from a distance. Pay attention to its body language and movements. How does it react to your presence?

2. Invitation to Connect: Slowly approach the horse, but watch its reactions carefully. If it turns away, move in a different direction and invite it to follow you by opening your body and adopting a welcoming posture.

2. Build Respect and Trust: When the horse starts following you, maintain a gentle but steady rhythm in your movements. Show confidence and clarity in your behavior. Make sure to balance closeness and space so the horse feels safe.

3. Reflection: After the exercise, take time to reflect on what you observed. How did the horse respond to you? Where did you notice uncertainty or clarity in your leadership style?

Exercise 14

Strengthen inner peace and serenity

This exercise helps you build a harmonious connection with the horse while strengthening your own inner calm and serenity.

1. Find calm: Stand next to the horse, either freely or held by the halter, and close your eyes for a moment. Take a deep breath in through your nose and slowly exhale through your mouth. Focus on calming your breath and keeping it even.

2. Synchronize breathing: Open your eyes and watch the horse. Try to sync your breathing with the horse's movements, like the rise and fall of its chest or its steps if it walks beside you.

3. Steady rhythm: Make sure your breath stays calm and steady, even if the horse moves. If you notice your breath becoming uneven, pause for a moment and return to your calm rhythm.

4. Wordless communication: With a relaxed breath, try to communicate with the horse through your breathing. Let the calm and peace you create with your breath flow over to the horse. Notice if the horse becomes calmer or more relaxed.

5. Reflection: After the exercise, reflect on how your breath affected your mental and emotional state. Write down whether the horse changed its behavior when you consciously controlled your breathing. What changes did you notice?

Exercise 15

Emotions in the Mirror

This is a deep and powerful exercise that helps you connect your emotions with the behavior of the horse. It offers valuable insights into your own emotional experience and how it affects your surroundings.

1. Centering: Start in a quiet room or near the horse. Sit or stand comfortably, close your eyes, and take deep breaths in and out.

2. Identify the topic: Think of an issue that's currently on your mind. Let the thoughts come up without judging or trying to change them. Just notice what's there.

3. Feel the emotions: Recognize the emotions connected to this topic. Maybe you feel fear, sadness, frustration, or something else. Allow yourself to fully feel and accept these emotions.

4. Observe the horse: Open your eyes and focus on the horse. Stand or sit nearby without trying to influence it. Watch how the horse reacts to your presence and emotional energy: Does it get restless, curious, or more relaxed?

5. Reflection: Take some time after the exercise to think about and write down what you observed:

____ [1]

Chapter 18
Willingness to Change

Choosing not to change or to allow change in your life is a decision that fundamentally shapes your life. Are you willing to break out of your comfort zone and grow, or would you rather stay as you are? Both choices come with a price: If nothing changes, everything stays the same. Leaving behind something familiar, like being disconnected from your feelings, can feel scary at first, but in the long run, it can be freeing and transformative.

Reconnecting with yourself can be painful at first. Dissociating from your own feelings was, unconsciously, a protective mechanism against a difficult or traumatic experience you couldn't handle in the past. But right now, you have the chance to come back to yourself. The following three exercises are designed to help you open your subconscious to that.

Exercise 16

Everything stays the same

Sit down with a sheet of paper and a pen. Calm yourself and think about your current situation: What price do you pay if you don't change anything? Write honestly about what it costs you to keep things as they are. Consider all levels: your position in the company, your physical health, your emotional well-being, your financial situation, the company's financial situation and your influence on it, as well as other life areas that are important to you right now.

Exercise 17

Everything will be different

Now take a second sheet of paper. Think about what would happen if you made a change: What would be the price for this change? Look at all levels here too and focus on the things you can actually change.

Exercise 18

Price comparison

Transfer your "costs" from the first two exercises onto a new sheet of paper. Arrange them in two columns opposite each other. Let the comparison sink in. If you notice you forgot something on either side, just add it.

Don't force a decision, take your time. Keep revisiting your list: Which price is higher?

My price for not changing – My price for changing

My price for not changing	My price for changing	
		1
		2
		3
		4
		5
		6
		7
		8
		9
		10
		11

Chapter 19
Finding Strength in Peace

Each individual in society is more called upon than ever to grow and evolve. I am convinced of this: We are facing great challenges on a global level, and everyone can, may, and should contribute by seeking peace within themselves, radiating it outward, and drawing strength from it for themselves and others.

The following exercises are designed to help you open yourself to your inner peace, to feel it, and to experience it more and more often.

Exercise 19

Exploring Resistance

Imagine that starting today, you consciously connect with all your hidden or suppressed parts of your personality. Tune into yourself: Do you feel any resistance to this idea? If so, what kind? Write them down and then take a step back to observe them calmly from a bird's-eye view.

Exercise 20

Recognizing Inner Conflict

A wonderful exercise for expressing and processing inner conflict is the "clay journal." Each day or week, create a small artwork out of clay that reflects your current feelings and thoughts.

When you sit down to sculpt, take a moment to calm yourself so you can fully focus on your emotions. Then take some soft clay in your hands and spontaneously shape whatever comes to mind – a figure, a symbol, or an abstract form. Let your feelings guide your hands and allow them to flow into the form.

Looking back, can you find words for it? If so, write them down here.

Audio Journal Entry 1:

Audio Journal Entry 2:

Audio Journal Entry 3:

Audio Journal Entry 4:

Exercise 21

Choosing Peace

Draw two pictures of yourself: Start with a picture that shows the parts of yourself you're still at odds with. You can even assign those parts to certain areas of your body, based on how they feel. Then draw a second picture of yourself where you're completely at peace with who you are.

Hang both pictures side by side – ideally somewhere you'll see them before going to sleep and when you wake up. Every day, consciously connect with these images and decide again and again which one you want to focus on today.

Write down your decision.

Day 1:

Day 2:

Day 3:

Day 4:

Day 5:

Day 6:

Day 7:

Day 8:

Chapter 20
Taking the first step

"How is that supposed to help me in my situation?"

"Fear? A real man doesn't get scared."

"How is the company situation ever going to improve if I just can't find any employees?"

"My kids are sick because of me – are you serious?"

"Spare me the psycho stuff. You think I'm crazy or what?"

"I've already tried so many things, none of it worked."

"Inner peace isn't exactly going to help me get new clients."

"You can't do anything different with these employees anyway."

"I am who I am."

"As long as those at the top don't change anything, nothing will change for me either."

"You're powerless against fate."

"You can't just talk your way into a fulfilled life."

"Some people just get lucky in life, others don't."

In my coaching work, I often hear objections like these. And I always say the same thing: everyone is free to make their own choices. Every single day, you get to decide whether you want to create something new, or keep making the same choices and living the same familiar reality.

To borrow a quote from Einstein:

The definition of insanity is doing the same thing over and over again and expecting different results.

No one can make the decision to change for you. Taking that step out of your comfort zone is something only you can do. You're responsible for your actions, own that responsibility and take the leap. It's never too late to take the first step.

A new life

Every step on the journey back to yourself brings you closer, to who you are, to your wishes, and to your needs. Writing this book has brought me closer to myself too. I'm writing these lines in Sri Lanka, where I originally planned to stay just a few weeks to finish the book. But I soon realized how much my body and soul were healing in this environment, so I stayed longer.

I'm finally allowing myself to open up to a dream I've had for many years: traveling the world. I never dared to do it before, my fears about money and all the what-ifs were just too strong. But working on this book made me realize this is my path, and everything else will fall into place.

My feelings are my compass. Ever since I made this decision, my life has felt lighter than ever before. Here in Sri Lanka and Thailand, I'm finding new strength, to keep helping others and to guide them on their own journey back to themselves AND to beautiful places around the world, far away from mass tourism.

I wish you all the best as you discover your own path within. And if you'd like support, I'm here for you, happy to walk with you on your journey to inner strength and authenticity, whether online or in person. And if you're up for it, with a horse co-trainer once I'm back in Germany, probably starting in early 2026.

Wishing you all the best on your journey - Tanja Gruber

About the author

Tanja Gruber was born in 1968 in the heart of Upper Bavaria and has lived through more than most people could fit into one lifetime. Countless accidents, surgeries, and near-death experiences, along with months-long journeys to faraway places like Thailand, Sri Lanka, and Mexico, have shaped her into both a curious world traveler and someone deeply connected to her roots.

Over the years, she's explored a wide range of methods focused on personal growth and trauma healing. She trained as a sports massage therapist, Watsu practitioner, and reflexology therapist. She also completed training in dance and expressive therapy, is a certified NLP practitioner, and holds a diploma in personality training. On top of that, she completed advanced training in identity-oriented psychotrauma therapy (IoPT) and has now taken part in or facilitated thousands of IoPT intention sessions. She worked through many of her own issues in horse-assisted therapy, including sessions with Christine Huß-Doliana.

Her experiences have taught Tanja how powerful it can be to face deep inner issues with courage. With empathy, sensitivity, and years of hands-on experience, she helps people reconnect with themselves, find inner clarity, and tap into their own strength. She's deeply grateful every time someone places their trust in her and finds more peace and success in life with her support.

By her side since 2014: her Noriker gelding Pascha, who has touched the hearts of countless people through their work with horses. Tanja has been self-employed since 1994, writing books, professional articles, and ghostwriting other people's stories. For her, writing has always been a way to share insights with the world, and to open up new perspectives where none seemed possible.

You can learn more about Tanja Gruber at:

www.tanjagruber.de and www.tanjagruber.tentary.com

on LinkedIn (Tanja Gruber) and on

Instagram (tanjagruber_official).

www.ingramcontent.com/pod-product-compliance
Lightning Source LLC
Chambersburg PA
CBHW041302210926
51847CB00010B/118
* 9 7 8 3 9 0 3 5 2 1 7 5 9 *